Through A Distant Lens: Travel Poems

Collected and Edited

by Sheryl Clough

Through A Distant Lens: Travel Poems

An Anthology by Write Wing Publishing

Whidbey Island, Washington

Copyright © 2014 Write Wing Publishing

Poets hold the rights to their individual works.

All rights reserved.

ISBN-10: 1495933423
ISBN-13: 978-1495933424

PHOTO CREDITS

Page 4: Buddhist Temple "Tiger's Nest" at 14,000', Himalayas, Bhutan – Vincent J. Tomeo

Page 27: Mother and Child, Costa Rica – Sandra Hubbard

Page 47: Kells Priory, County Kilkenny, Ireland – Bill H. McGeary

Page 70: Frozen Hair, Chiseled Chin, on The Thames, London, England – Sculpture by Emily Young
Vincent J. Tomeo

Front Cover: Mural at Small Town Coffee, Kapa'a, Kauai, Hawaii – Sheryl Clough

Back Cover: Editor at Giants Causeway, County Antrim, Northern Ireland
Bill H. McGeary

CONTENTS

I	Departure		1
II	Continental Drift		4
	Ann Curran ... There, Not Here		5
	Judith Adams ... Across the Universe		6
	Joe Massingham ... Taj Mahal		8
	Linda Beeman ... Kingfisher Dreams		10
	Judith O'Connell Hoyer ... Cape of Good Hope		11
	Russ Stratton ... The E & O		12
	Ellaraine Lockie ... A Montanan in Bali		13
	Diane Stone ... Last Night's Chicken Curry		14
	Vincent J. Tomeo ... Iguazu Falls		15
	Rosemary Volz ... Passage		16
	Catharine Bramkamp ... A Circle of Stones		18
	Patricia L. Goodman ... Morning in Mongolia		19
	Suzanne Ondrus ... From Africa to Russia		20
	Gelia Dolcimascolo ... Sayonara		22
	Debra Marquart ... Wild Thyme		24
	Gabrielle Baalke ... Tuscany		26
III	Snapshots from the Road		27
	Ann Howells ... Moving On		28
	Marianne Patty ... Our Lady of the Street		29
	Lois Parker Edstrom ... Yellowstone Park, 1948		30
	Gelia Dolcimascolo ... La Jolla (The Jewel)		31
	Nasus ... Road Trip Rerun		32
	K. Andrew Turner ... Converse		34
	Vanessa Garcia ... Key West		35

	Margo Davis ... Travelling 45 South From Dallas	36
	Brett Foster ... Itinerant Sonnet, Relaxed	37
	Gail Denham ... Treasured Journeys, A Memory Jumble	38
	Linda Beeman ... Driving Home	40
	Barbra Nightingale ... At the Launderette	42
	Teddy Norris ... Barging in Burgundy	43
	Debra Marquart ... Traveling With Guitar	44
	Scott T. Starbuck ... Backroads	45

2014 Write Wing Publishing Poetry Prize:

	Carol Alexander ... Piazza San Marco, 1980	46
IV	**Borders Less Defined**	47
	Ron Thompson ... A Brief Visit to Heaven	48
	Ann Boutte' ... Last Visit to Walnut Street	51
	Ann Curran ... Poet Mugged	52
	Ann Curran ... Catching the Blues	53
	Virginia Chase Sutton ... Of A Transient Nature	54
	Vanessa Garcia ... Roadtrip	56
	Bill Carpenter ... Lunar Winter	57
	Calvin Ahlgren ... Flight	58
	Gail Denham ... Cornelius and the Big Blow	60
	Scott T. Starbuck ... Remembering Chief Charlie DePoe Who Loved Trains	62
	Peter Ludwin ... Reading *Conquest of the Incas* in the Cirque, Central Peru	63
	Sheila Nickerson ... Detour: Driving North on I-5	64
	Beth Hutmacher ... Fire	65

	Carol Davis ... We Did Not Come for the Birds	66
	Diane Stone ... Leaving	67
	Michaelsun Knapp ... Great Wave Off Oklahoma	68
V	Interior Frames	70
	Ann Boutte' ... Adventure	71
	Ann Howells ... Housesitting on Looking Glass Lane	72
	Pamela A. Smith ... Boat Launch	73
	Lois Parker Edstrom ... Yesterday's Light	74
	Jed Myers ... A Breath Before Doubt	76
	John Baalke ... Dutchman's Trail, Superstition Wilderness	77
	Ilene Adler ... Destination: The Fallow Land	78
	Ilene Adler ... Destination: The Fertile Land	79
	Bill Carpenter ... Unlikely Journeys	80
	Bill Carpenter ... Antelope Canyon, Arizona	81
	Mark Hart ... Hiking with my Son in the Grand Canyon	82
	Beth Hutmacher ... Story	83
	Patricia L. Goodman ... Black Bear Hunt, Olympia, Washington	84
	Gretchen Diemer ... Dream on Aitutaki	86
	Sheila Nickerson ... On Transplanting the Poppies	88
	Karla Linn Merrifield ... *A Hui Ho*	89
VI	Arrival	90
VII	Poet Notes	91
VIII	About Write Wing Publishing	103

for Theresa, Bill, and Snickers, with love

I Departure

For as long as humans have inhabited Earth, they have traveled. Prehistoric humans crossing the Bering Land Bridge on foot to reach North America; Vikings sailing their warships far and wide; Marco Polo's Asiatic forays; de Rozier and d'Arlandes going aloft in the first untethered hot air balloon flight: history regales us with accounts of movement over land, upon the sea, and through the air. Via writings, drawings, petroglyphs and photographs, many travelers have sought to define their adventures for audiences of the less-traveled.

Martha Gellhorn wrote, "You define your own horror journey, according to your taste. My definition of what makes a journey wholly or partially horrible is boredom." Certainly the poets in this volume have suffered many indignities of the road, but nowhere in the writing does boredom surface as one of them. These poems are remarkable for their artistry, their passion, and their wide-ranging perspectives. We listen awe-struck with Tomeo at the roaring Iguazu Falls; we grieve with Merrifield as she scatters her brother's ashes in Hawaii; when Denham's Cornelius soars aloft in the tornado, we fly alongside him, exulting in his wind-powered joy.

Demonstrating that the physical body has no monopoly on movement, some of these poets experience what Lois Parker Edstrom has called "interior travels." Thus, Ann Boutte' is content with the adventures lived from the contours of her easy chair, and Pamela Smith pilots a skiff woven only from the threads of her vivid imaginings.

Preferring the actual skiff to the imagined, the iconic late Northwest poet Nelson Bentley was fond of defining a romantic as someone who, upon seeing a boat of any kind, would jump aboard and sail away. The poets in this collection are not short of waterborne tales; a heartbreaking example is Volz' scene of Irish emigration, "Passage." For a less romantic representation of the boat journey, Curran renders "Catching the Blues."

The darker facets of human exploration are not neglected here. Stratton's "E & O" gives a laser-focused glimpse of colonial exploitation, while Ondrus laments loss and racism in Russia. Sutton's Buenos Aires is rendered as the polar opposite of glamorous through a series of precise word-snapshots. Knapp takes the ekphrastic poem to a new height by juxtaposing tsunami-borne destruction in Japan with the destruction of First Nations cultures in North America.

An instructor in a long-ago backpacking course told the class that given the choice between packing more food and more camera equipment, he would choose the camera gear every time. If I met him today, I would tell him all he needs to take along is a notebook and pencil, for creating poems that would live long after the completion of his journey. The poets whose visions enrich this volume already know that, and as reader-viewers, we are the lucky beneficiaries of their creative knowledge.

                                        Sheryl Clough
                                        Whidbey Island, Washington
                                        February 2014

II Continental Drift

There, Not Here

Funny how your mind takes you somewhere else.
Lipstick to lip, I switch from my bedroom
in Pittsburgh to a cottage in Ireland.

I stand before the Dolans' dim mirror.
I can't see without a light there or here.
Will have to go into the frigid bathroom.

There, not here. But wonder how my head went
with a mere lift of arm to lip from here --
without a ticket or frisking -- to there.

-- Ann Curran

Across the Universe

Strange to wake with this song in my head
"Nothing's gonna change my world."

I cannot ignore such a reveille.
Everything is changing our world:

war, revolution, nefarious banks,
fanatical ideology and

children manipulating icons,
toxic as mustard gas.

A sobering list,
the world in worrisome flux but

the young are setting off across the globe
for the sake of someone else.

People peeling away prejudice,
victims in dialogue with perpetrators,

dew mirroring the world at dawn,
and the curve of the moon

swelling the harvest.
So long as there are hallowed hills

to hike towards and no matter what
cruelty exists in yourself,

red and yellow songs are in the holly tree,
salvation in a stranger's face and

all across the universe surprising arrival
at the community table.

Though troublesome, we are
sitting together.

Slowly, very slowly, something is going
to change our world.

-- Judith Adams

Taj Mahal

I

Mumtaz Mahal, at one with Sarasvati,
lying in scarlet silken shroud with saffron sash,
cymbals on your fingers and bells on your toes,
your body colder than the coldest marble,
sleeping now the sleep of liberation,
lying where you are
because
the nearness of our children
adds to your pleasure.

For now,

whisper to me from your resting place,
hidden by the shining light,
beyond the veil of night.

Pool of white,
pool of light,
pool of life,
mirroring
a life of love.

The pool, a catchment of the life of Mother Ganges,
a pool that lies still until you need that life again.
And sometimes when the light is right
I fancy I see reflected in the pool
that fine golden thread that links my heart to yours.

I promise I will join you when Allah so decrees.

II

Coming back from an errand for Allah
the other day I was passing near Agra
and thought I'd stop and visit you.
How I wished I hadn't!
How sad it was to see our earthly
resting place so distressed.
Its alabaster skin has faded to
a sallow yellow,
gentle welcome boards replaced by
pollution count displays.
The sweetly flowing Yamuna
on whose banks we used to sit
has become a morass of shit,
an open drain lined with solid waste.
The decline of water height and flow
exposing the supports for our death beds,
threatening to cast us in the mire
like unremembered beggars, holding
out our hands for alms from those
misled into coming to marvel at our
sometime Paradise on earth.

-- Joe Massingham

Kingfisher Dreams

surfacing from dreams
can be exhausting – a slow
ascent from deep within

this morning I traveled back
from a Ch'ing dynasty world
caressed by smooth silks
elaborate kingfisher feather jewelry
clouds of incense

homeless for all that
seeking shelter in two-dimensional
apartments stacked one atop another
a Confucian advent calendar
shielding my concubine self

under someone's protection
I reverberated to cymbal ching
light pressure of fingers at my temples
inhaled fragrance of chilies and rice
inside a pampered cage

breaking the day I remember
Pu-yi's second wife walking away
from their compound
tossing her umbrella aside
welcoming the rain

-- Linda Beeman

Cape of Good Hope

Visitors stand on the scruffy head
of the promontory. They squint at
wind-beating caravels that sped
Sir Bart Diaz and his Portuguese
deck-mates around Africa's salty

cone in 1488. The place where
storm-lost hulls lie pickled on
the ocean floor. Now, down the bony
nape to the thrilling riff of tides
so full of themselves.

Dolphins blossom in their garden
park. Whales flirt with passing
ships. A forest of brown kelp
grows on the chest of the sea
and cabochon clusters of lustrous

blue mussels shine at the throats
of granite rocks. Toothless
ostriches bat sand from their
bulging eyes and swallow stones
to settle their stomachs. Baboon

troops scoot over spiny fynbos
with their bare bums sticking in
the air. The monkey mothers
groom their young in public
while Fagin dads school the ruff-

necked lads in the art of picking
trippers' pockets, then
scamper off to stuff their cheeks
with apples and oranges atop
a rented BMW or red Ferrari.

-- Judith O. Hoyer

The E & O

We lunch on beetroot salad, eggs mayonnaise,
Gazing past the hotel cat, so curiously hungry,
First at Butterworth, the purple Malayan mainland,
Then moving down the Straits of Panang, azure,
Filled with fishing sampans,
The light shimmering, equatorial heat gathering,
Coming closer to the sea wall which bounds
Our paradise, a patio of clipped hedge and lawn,
Potted bougainvilleas, coxcombs,
An emerald pool about which silent
Chinese waiters, white-jacketed,
Their movements subdued,
Quiet as their black slippers,
Signal a garden undisturbed as
We turn back to our guests and
Speak of tennis games, of shopping,
And of our comprehension of Empires.

-- Russ Stratton

A Montanan in Bali

Seated on an outdoor toilet
segregated in its own tiny house
A trough of water beside me waits with ladle
to be dipped into and splashed onto body parts
that expect the dry rub of paper
instead of a wet left hand

In this land where time reverses
my chest tightens into a crystal ball
A diorama of a young girl who sneaked
downstairs after her aunt had gone to bed
Sporadic steps so it sounded
like the old farmhouse stretching its legs
From the kitchen she carried a Bauer pottery bowl
whose contents would mark an oak outside
before she placed it back in the cupboard

It wasn't the summer stench that kept her
from the outhouse at night
But neither were the spiders deterred
The long black legs of fear and the belly
of shame still crawl over the girl
forty years and several countries later
Though no webbed witness surrounds her
here in this *way say*

A knot loosens and the farm scene,
like a funeral balloon, is set free to fade away
In its wake lives a country-wide custom forbidding
the touch of people or food with the left hand
The Balinese fare better than the ranch hands
who ate breakfast eggs beaten in a Bauer bowl

-- Ellaraine Lockie

---

way say = toilet

Last Night's Chicken Curry

Last night's chicken curry was a Nepali version
whose ancient aroma clung like fragrant vines
to every corner of our home.
Rafts of ardent spices floated
across the dull Western heartland of our kitchen.
Forget meatloaf and peas, jello and peaches.
Forget chicken breasts baked in cream.
Forget steamed fish and peeled potatoes.

Asian history and flavors transported us
to a cold mountain village where the smooth hands
of beautiful women, dark-haired in gracious saris,
stand like tall sultanas stirring sauce
and bubbly revolutions in shiny copper pots.
Crowded streets erupt in glossy golds and reds,
so much pushing and pulling, buying and selling.
Children and their pups run through muddy puddles;
white goats bleat and kick;
impatient bearded men on crimson pillows
await their favorite curry.

Ours had morsels of chicken, threads of saffron,
golden cumin, fenugreek seeds, garum marsala,
the amber soul of turmeric, plump garlic cloves diced
into white cubes of heat that clung to our palms,
sliced onions thin as damsel wings,
topaz of ginger, rough cardamom, and coriander leaves.
A perfect sauce, this Biblical creation.
Such a passion of eating, no grace could do it justice.

-- Diane Stone

Iguazu Falls

Sounds cascade ripple down
staircases of jungle green and granite
like melting wedding cakes

Thunder surges sprinkles blessings
Might of planet sings
Mist blankets panoramic view like angels rising
Sun engages dew to veil light in white blue clouds
wondrous natural world explodes billows forward

Hear the earth roar

-- Vincent J. Tomeo

Passage

And so we took the train from Donnybrook.
You sat so close to me that I could feel
The bulk of you rise and fall being too
Restless to sleep you stretched your neck
And cleared your throat, so unaccustomed
To sitting still and watching the passage of time.
Silent hours together – as intimate as our bed.

When the last of the sun filtered through the car,
I noticed how worn your coat sleeves were,
Though it was a proper coat, being Kerry wool
And your father's finest. And I
In Sheelagh's shiny shoes, feeling the imposter.
In my haste I had forgotten my gloves and I
Hid my roughened hands but you grabbed them
Searching for the gold band so you could turn it round
   and round.
For good luck, I thought.
You said God owed us a favor.

A holy card from your mother was stuffed in your
   pocket,
A colored picture of our Savior's crucifixion
Though we needed no reminders of suffering
Being a tribe so prone to disaster, so beautifully
   fashioned for defeat.
But we had sworn to leave those ghosts behind
And let the trowel rust in the field.

Emptying the heart is hard work,
The alder trees down by the stream,
The worthless teapot my mother treasured
Graves covered with earth and ferns
And you making the circle complete
A loving son who grew weary of doors without
   keyholes.

I took out the bread and cheese and we ate like thieves
While the train labored through forsaken cities filled
   with hungry souls.
Getting off the train, I tripped on my borrowed boots
But before the ground greeted me, your hands were
   there
And you joked that I would surely miss my country
   brogues.

The ship was waiting at the dock, bathed in moonlight
I felt empowered by the calmness of the water and
   your face
We knew not what lay ahead – Canaan or Calvary?
Yet of two things I was certain,
I had married a good man and my feet would always
   hurt.

-- Rosemary Volz

A Circle of Stones

Rocks circle the computer monitor
As if someone else
Carefully placed them

To balance the humming, the imperceptible.

A blue Faberge egg from Moscow
A fantastic dragon from Vietnam
A metal scarab from Luxor

And the rocks, smooth
Rough – striated in red, purple and gold
Slipped into a pocket
Site specific

Mark Twain was horrified at
The sanctimonious pilgrims
Who stole chunks of the holy land
Subtracting from there
Piling up here

Limestone from the Valley of the Kings
A smooth stone from Santa Barbara
I move them around
Categorize them
Write about them
Like right here.

This one is from Ireland
A land filled with stones
Laboriously collected
And pushed upright to last

Pretty much forever.

-- Catharine Bramkamp

Morning in Mongolia

Her eyes followed me
as I struggled, shivering,
from my sleeping bag,
hands too cold to function,
embarrassed tears
sneaking down my face.

She had come
to wake us and light our stove,
but quickly detected my agony,
unprepared as I was
for the frigid, high-desert nights.

She came toward me,
took my freezing hands in hers,
opened her shirt,
and pressed them
against the warm skin of her body,
whispering soothing words
in a tongue I did not understand.

Tears flowed faster.
I leaned my head on her shoulder,
as skin warmth returned life
not only to useless hands,
but to a heart
that had forgotten
how compassion needs no language.

-- Patricia L. Goodman

From Africa to Russia

It's time to go back to Russia,
where I can pack myself with boiled *pelmeni*
those bundles of pork and chicken,
where I can smear gobs of Siberian white honey
over my sauna reddened skin,
sink myself into a *vatrushka's* cheese center,
and stare hours through snow
at the pretty, red place,
winding my eyes up to St. Basil's
golden dome.

It's time to go back to Russia with heartbreak,
back for solidification, mending, filling.
Where shall I place him this time?
In a troika, in a samovar,
in a loom or among the wild pack
of dogs gathered outside the metro?

Mangy, ungroomed, listless the dogs lie,
waiting for kindness –
a dropped chicken bone, a *pirozhki's* end
or a greasy napkin.
It's here I would place him,
out in the open, where everyone
passes by.

But it would be dangerous.
He'd likely be pummeled
for being black.
And his beautiful wide nose
would be smashed.
His hair in clumps on the concrete
and his thick soft lips
cracked, pouring forth no words,
but color – red, red, red.

And I wish I could have understood him better,
grasped the drawn out A's
of his *Moore'* language and poured
beautiful paragraphs into his ears.
But something wasn't there,
and so among the mango,
karate and nere trees I couldn't stay.
I cannot spell it.

There were too few deep wells
between us – and humans are 90% water.
And camels can only store water
for a specified number of days.

The cowrie shells had to be spoken.
They spelled come undone.

-- Suzanne Ondrus

Sayonara

soft
toast
touch-move
konnichiwa
tie-dye

I carry your words
on my flight home,
moments I capture
with my butterfly net of a pen,
insert onto the page
one word at a time –
mementos of you at ten.

soft
you whispered,
jiggling the skin on my hand,
caressing my cheek

toast!
your focaccia clinked
my wine glass mid-air
both of us giggled

touch-move
the chess game
I lost to you

konnichiwa
the word I overheard
during your Japanese lesson

tie-dye
the answer you gave me
for the crossword puzzle
we pored over last night

soft
toast
touch-move
konnichiwa
tie-dye

sayonara

-- Gelia Dolcimascolo

Wild Thyme

I took the photographs as the other poets
fell backwards into wild thyme, too worried
about appearing the tourist or ruining my clothes

in the phryngana, the zone between mountain
and sea, wood and water. On the rented boat
to Antiparos, as the others slipped into wet suits,

pulled on squeaky flippers, rolled into azure depths
with Panayotis, the marine biologist, I stayed
on the moored boat with whiskery Captain Giorgos

nursing my salty old grudges against water.
On the south shore of the island, when invited
to sing into the mouth of the sea caves that echo

the ancient world back, I had only this pop tune
to offer (I can't bear to name it). Between Lefkes
and Marpissa, where the Byzantine trail empties

down to the sea, when the old man with hair
like a wild bird's nest and a toothless collapsing
chin saw me, an American, enter the chapel

he guarded, he shouted, *Ah, George Bush!*
and my only response was, *I didn't do it!*
(meaning, vote for him) which made all

the other Americans laugh. At Marathi,
where the mountain opens to marble quarries
so translucent that the Venus de Milo,

the temples on Delos, and Napoleon's tomb
are carved from it, as the guide distributed
the headlamps for our underground excursion,

he had to ask, *Now, is anyone here claustrophobic?*
And I had to answer, *Well, yes,* because
I would never depend upon tourists

to pull my limp and breathless body
from any dark crevasse. So I guarded
the entrance as the others descended,

sat back to study the guidebooks.
Did you know that 150,000 slaves mined
these quarries. They say a bas relief

above one opening depicts Pan cavorting
with Nymphs. Did you know the thyme
that grows on this mountainside feeds

bees that make rare, wild honey, the color
of amber. Aromatic and savory, they say,
with the taste of white pepper, dates, and fruit.

-- Debra Marquart

Tuscany

We were here for Easter, when the bells rang out
and the countryside laid down its Italian
to become Faithful, Merciful, Love.

We walked together from the stables
down the little lane. *Pranzo di Pasqua*
and the entire village gathered.

Later, the daughters of the Milanese father teach
the young boy English and the boy reads me
numbers in his rounded native French.

Lentamente, slowly, the trimmings of the olive trees
burn in the fire, warming the room where we are
  gathered,
warming more than the room, more than the country
  of Italy.

-- Gabrielle Baalke

III SNAPSHOTS FROM THE ROAD

Moving On

In my rearview mirror Dallas fades.
Skyscrapers become Lego constructions;
Reunion Tower, a dandelion gone to seed.
S' maze solidifies into a thumbprint
on the glass.

The Cowboys are playing; trucks stand
grill-to-tailgate around Loop 12.
Neon blinks on, and at the farmer's market
an elderly woman haggles in Spanish
for the last basket of tomatillos.

Phoenix, where I am bound, materializes –
less like Brigadoon from Scottish mists,
than Petra carved from red sand. Sunlight
bounces from rooftop and walkway
in palpable waves.

Even now, shoe stores order
elegant sandals (size 6 ½), bookstores
expand poetry sections, grocers stock up
on Ben & Jerry's Funky Monkey
as they await my arrival.

-- Ann Howells

Our Lady of the Street

She shuffles down
George Washington Boulevard,
a lace mantilla on a frizzle
of her see-through hair,
her memories locked away
in a cracked leather pocketbook.

She stutter-steps in worn-out shoes
up the steep stairs of the old church.

Stained-glass Jesus watches her progress,
flaming heart exposed,
hands studded with nails.
Mother Mary stands on the dirt lawn,
arms outstretched with lopped-off fingers,
a smile on her face.
Someone has spray painted
unrepeatable words
on her cement gown.

Occasional cars pass.
Drivers mouth words
Mother Mary ignores.

Papers swirl and lift around
broken bottles and used syringes.
Empty buildings languish now
their doorway-people
sleeping it off
somewhere else.

She continues her painful ascent
up the stairs of her broken world.

-- Marianne Patty

Yellowstone Park, 1948

Memory stalks the years,
a distant traveler scuffing up
the dust of nostalgia –
a handmade Indian doll,
scrolled silver belt buckle,
an Old West saloon,
lightning lassoing the night sky
and I a dusty ten year old,
in the back seat of the Plymouth.

That night scrubbed in an old iron tub,
Yardley's English Lavender Soap,
clean pajamas, I hear wind rumpling
the pines, cones plunking
on the shingled roof of the cabin,
smooth log walls, butterscotch gold,
and knots like owl's eyes that see
everything. I remember that night
settled deep in a feather bed,
the line-fresh memory
I've used to measure comfort
for over sixty years –

crisp white sheets.

-- Lois Parker Edstrom

La Jolla (The Jewel)

> *Last night*
> *I dreamed*
> *of glass shards,*
> *hands and wrists*
> *splintered with pain,*
> *every twist a reminder*
> *of our first parting.*

You and I meander
down Prospect Avenue,
dart in and out
of glass galleries,
curious, not serious,
enjoying the simple act
of window shopping,
pause to admire a glasswork
which symbolizes our bond:
"Just Friends."

Yesterday, California was home.
Now I've become a tourist
in the land of cliff caves and beaches.

Once again,
we must separate,
just friends who dwell
three thousand miles apart,
fused by our past,
temporally rejoined
by the present
in La Jolla.

-- Gelia Dolcimascolo

Road Trip Rerun

The road rumble strip
rattles my brain

the energy snack mix
has turned rancid with time

blooming sage on the roadside
helps sweeten the air

red stones that I gathered
feel smooth in my hands

I found them at Arches
before we were told

The Government is closing
we're locking the gate

get your ass out of here
before it's too late

on our exit drive out
we stopped at a site

the doors to the rest rooms
were locked up tight

U. S. Rangers blocked the trail
that was on our trip plan

I always thought
this was everyone's land

apparently I didn't
quite understand

the true meaning of freedom
when it comes to *our land*

is controlled by our leaders
who ought to be canned

-- Nasus

Converse

If the tan Converse dangling
up there,
on those very wires
we ourselves use
to converse,
could tell a story,
perhaps they would mention
how they'd managed to fly,
break gravity
like I did recently
to come here,
to this street in St. John's
Portland, OR;
or perhaps it would
be a converse story
and say that they've been
hanging out
forever there to make
me wonder,
while I sip chai
across the street.

-- K. Andrew Turner

Key West

It's hot
even through
UV-protected
tinted windows.

Tar melting
like black-pharaoh-ink
and sinking
They say
we'll be underwater
soon

You could say
all coastlines
are the same
smoldering vastness
and the smell
of sometimes rot

Or you could say
this one is different
this old bridge
beside us for 7 miles
once a blueprint
hinting towards home
Cuba
that phantom limb

Migrant birds
marooned
and stuck
in the melting tar

-- Vanessa Garcia

Travelling 45 South From Dallas

An eighteen-wheeler on my
twilight right
fills an entire lane
until he hugs the divider
which makes me drift
instinctively
to my left, where oversized
tires with whirling
red hubcaps hypnotize me
until I look up to read
the worry lines on the license plate
staring me down. This *Great Dane*
carries baling wire
eager to roll off
on its own chaotic plight.
When I lift my foot
from the gas, a *Red Bull*
delivery truck snorts
on my trunk.
In the moment it takes
to drop my racing speed
to 75 – two bats
of an eyelash –
everything folds in and I fall
prey to a *Skinny Cow*
ambling right out of nowhere.
As brake lights flicker like
lightning bugs at dusk,
a mason-jar mist
hovers then drops, hemming
this traveler's fate.

-- Margo Davis

Itinerant Sonnet, Relaxed

*Who wants to have to count on his fingers
the rest of the days of his life?*

Today I've run away to Marathon,
unobservant of anything important.
Don't underestimate the pelican
above the road's shoulder like an iron-on,
suspended, wings dipping.

Left at Lazy Lizard's, past Addesley
House, turtle hospital, Curry Hammock Park,
till dining at Burdines chiki-tiki bar
atop the marina.
Tab in a mouse-trap so it won't blow away.

Deep in the Keys, the breezes barely stir
groups of fishermen fishing for grouper
off a bridge. Peace is a caballero,
charging full speed toward the glad undertow.

A couple keeps water in Tupperware
for their retriever.
Just leave it be,

as we bite the pith of what this place is,
at the world's edge: an ecstatic stasis.

-- Brett Foster

Treasured Journeys, A Memory Jumble

We had tea and succulent pastries at Betty's
Café in York, a refuge for WWII airmen, where
they came to dance and forget war for an evening.

Walked the surround walls in Chester;
strode the aisle where Princess Di
made her long journey into the Firm.

Walked over church stones covering
old greats; hiked through broken
castles; went again and again to Thursday
market day in Abergavenny, Wales.

Trains and buses took us to London War
Museum, and to holocaust remembrance
in Leon, France (once Gestapo headquarters),
tears blinding our eyes on departure.

Tea shops (finally a latte'); charity shops everywhere.
We purchase sweaters against July chill; fascinating
antiquarian bookstore; walked foot path from Gilwern
(once a military hospital), through pastures, climbed
    stiles,
greeted cows and sheep, photographed an ancient barn.

The mighty castle at Chepstow; where a glorious male
choir tape rang goodbyes to our final evening.
Blue-green Wales' air around us – air we could see,
feel, touch, smell as we waited another train.

Our journey, embedded in hearts, blending
into never-ending memories, bursting through
often, with blinding clarity of ducking under
ancient, blackened, decades-old ceilings.

Mrs. Jones' proper English breakfasts; bedrooms
three flights up; brilliant evening glow on last
standing wall of St. Mark's; ancient tobacconist
shop; red blossoms covering a wall to the roof.

Tintern Abbey, alone, quiet, in long-ago glory.

-- Gail Denham

Driving Home

Leaving green I think
as I depart my island tangle
cedar   blackberry   infinity of alders

cross the Sound   maneuver
Seattle's jangled arteries
congested anywhereness

follow a rising road
over granite-faced Snoqualmie
Chevy Silverados goad me forward

descend again into the Gorge
all wind   hot farmland
spiked by wind turbines

I would duel with given
a larger steed and a faithful
companion

the lines become apparent
they run dashed down the road
lay lambent   fences enclosing

field after field of tilled crops
tended by wheel line irrigators spraying
parallel arcs at thirsty plant rows

utility cables swag the low horizon
con trails stripe the sky
pull me east across 180 degrees of flat

until browns finally cede
to straggler scrub white pines
near Spokane   then Coeur d'Alene

where water begins to run quick
through cognac rocks and
mountains start to hug me again

-- Linda Beeman

At the Launderette (Dublin)

A simple thing: laundry
on a summer's day.
Go out the door, turn right
on Pearse Street. The Georgian
Launderette – Do it yourself,
three pound sixty.
A simple task
unless you're the type
where two plus two
never equals four,
no nothing so logical
as buy a paper, 50p.
Take it to read.
Slosh and suds
of your week's sweat
lifting out and away –
a fresher, drier you left behind –
unless you happen
on such a day as this
to take it into your head
to equate the *Daily Express*
with the *Irish Times,* dumped
as they were, in the wash,
bottom of the sack, realized
too late.
A simple task
on a summer's day,
wringing and whacking
your dripping clothes,
bits of paper flying about
while the management and passersby
stand and laugh at the Yank
free of charge.

-- Barbra Nightingale

Barging in Burgundy

We glide through water dark and smooth as green moiré'.
Outside our hotel barge, cathedral trees outline a river
    boulevard,
their limbs an arching symmetry of obeisance.

Like fallen clouds, puffs of sheep drift by in distant fields.
Drowsing horses dip and lift their heads, swish their tails
through the coppery shimmer of light on their flanks.

In hazy hills, a chateau's turrets float in lovely cliché'.
    Below its walls
the land unscrolls, diagrammed by looping rows of green
    on brown.
The earth-sky union promises bottled legends of rubies
    and golds.

And thus transported, we succumb to perfect ease
as villages send out their siren calls: how simple life
    could be –
tending vines, baking bread, raising goats for fragrant
    cheese!

Measured merely by our meals and languid passage
    through the locks,
time's sliding slows our hearts – Odysseans, drunk on
    bliss
and on the fond belief that we could never tire of this.

-- Teddy Norris

Traveling with Guitar

For you can travel with a screaming red rolling bag
and float unnoticed on conveyors, through terminals

or you can lug half a moose rack from Maine
to Minnesota, carry it like a broken wing through airports

as my friend Gro did, and draw only the curious touches
of children waiting at gates. But dare to travel with a guitar

and invite confessions from strangers in pinstripe suits
of garage band summers, invite winks, *gotcha* smiles,

and devil's horns *rock-on* gestures. Invite finger natches,
long tongue licks, and the rubberneck backward glances

to check if you are someone famous. To dare to travel
with a guitar is to mark yourself charismatic megafauna

of the airport terminal. Old friend, what else could I do
but carry you? I have stored you in closets, propped you

in corners, hunched over you late-nights, staring perplexed
at the mysteries of your neck. Body of my body, string

of my strings, see how the world began to hum and sing
that day at thirteen when I opened the big birthday box.

-- Debra Marquart

Backroads

A Native woman sent me 10 miles in the wrong direction
until I stood beside my idling gold Camry
measuring mud puddles with alders
as clearing sky reflected freedom her people lost
when white men arrived.

I imagined her roaring laughter
by a wood stove in December chill
as she spoke about trickster Coyote
and the steelheaded fisherman.

On backroads I saw nets
like abstracts of human faces
along swollen river
then friendly truthful elders
and a boat with raven bow.

Later, I drove south because
sometimes a man is so polluted by life
he needs a river big as the Columbia
to heal him.

-- Scott T. Starbuck

WINNER OF THE 2014 WRITE WING POETRY PRIZE

Piazza San Marco, 1980

Turn, and the gold-encrusted pigeons fly up at dusk,
fading to gray against the verdigris of manes. Come and
go day boats bearing the tall and blond, dark and svelte,
photographing horses, their labors stilled, chariot vague
    as air.

A girl in the piazza strains to catch the lisping local speech,
the curious eye of a waiter with his disaffected
dancer's stance; like the bronze horses, he'll give nothing
    warm and trembling away.

So the steeds, taking the last of the sun, raise fine heads
to a wind that sweeps the wide square from the Adriatic
Sea; the girl sips, shudders at the grappa's evil bite, for
which she's paid an unknowable sum, a clink of coins,
    a light touch on the palm.

From campo to campo, she's stalked by boys
with guidebook lore; but desire of horses is everywhere
    to see, and the pigeons roosting there.

See the beasts with gilded muzzles seemingly inclined,
a length apart, wondering at the giddiness in the air,
at the barques of traders losing their way, barred by
    darkness from the rank canal.

None can steal this feast of soft Venetian light, though
the horses think to guard forever the basilica, ignorant
of their fate, their final snorts and pawings rendered
by the girl, hatless at night, last seen searching
    for the bridge to her dim hotel.

-- Carol Alexander

IV BORDERS LESS DEFINED

A Brief Visit to Heaven

(what happened to Charles Bukowski?)

1
No pearly gates!
Creaking swinging doors, rusty hinges
Neon sign above, SUPER-SIZED:
"The Eye of the Needle."

2
Heaven!
A dingy, dinky tavern
Diminutive stage
Basketball, backboard-sized placard
On the back wall:
"Poetry Readings, Never Ending"

3
Pockmarked mail-carrier,
Poet reading
Poem stuffed, postal bag slung over
With recent collection:
"Pustules in Heaven, Prevarications & Other Aggravations"

4
Other poets, many poets
Too many poets
Lined up waiting to read
Just waiting to read!

5
Post Office Poet
Whiskey bottle drained
Flying with angel wings
Crashing near the bar
Like a wrecked car:
"Bring Me Another Beer Please."
A poem title announced from the new collection
Modulation, imitation
W. C. Fields droning speaking style.

6
Flying with angel wings
Empty bottle, "Copperhead-American Pale Ale"
Whistling, precisely missling
Past Post Office Poet's
Mastodonic poetry-stuffed head,
A churlish, churning poetry factory inside.

7
"What's HE doing HERE?
That loud, loutish drunkard over THERE?"
A recent arrival
To the Heavenly survival
DeMANded!
While piously pointing, perplexedly
At the Post Office Poet.

8
God, sipping at the Swilling Bar,
Her favorite, "Old Rasputin," deliciously on tap,
Sitting next to The Pious New Arrival,
Unbeknownst to him that she is God:
Responds delicately to his demand.
"That drunkard is my favorite poet,
Henry Chinaski,
And don't dare ask me, please,
To clodhopper boot him out!"

    9
How can there be "A Brief Visit to Heaven?"
To Eternity?
With another poem, with another reading
And another poem, and another reading

    10
The Poetry Merry-Go-Round chases its own tail
Round and round   Forever …

-- Ron Thompson

Last Visit to Walnut Street

The colors, now in neutral shades, are muted,
   drapes more formal with tassels and swags,
     ornaments more abundant and rococo,

still, the bones of my childhood
   home remain. It's the same two slate steps down
     to the glassed-in porch where we sat to dinner.

My father, gone twenty years, then
   the strong, handsome businessman, my mother,
     family ringmaster, gone, too. My brother, once tormenter

or co-conspirator, now co-keeper of our memories.
   The side yard once open to neighbors inviting
     games of ball tag and Red Rover has been fenced

and landscaped with fountains and hedges, a private
   oasis. In the spacious, beige living room,
     once a summery celadon, ghosts

of cocktail party-goers reconvene
   in clusters of conversation, ice
     tinkling in tumblers of bourbon and scotch,

wisps of smoke rising from glowing tips.
   Then a girl of ten, I perched on the stairway
     to steal glimpses between the balusters.

I step into the library, its dark paneling lightened,
   where my high school beau stole
     sweet kisses behind the closed door.

At the end of the visit, I leave behind
   our history coded in the walls, the bittersweet
     tableaus surrounded by the architectural pentimento.

-- Ann Boutte'

Poet Mugged

Four thugs from Armagh tripped into Galway.
Hanging around Eyre Square, they honed in on
Padraic O'Conaire, who shouts shyness,
bent over, hat plopped, feet tangled together.
The great poet who wrote only in Irish.
And, damn, if they didn't lop off his head.
It rolled around defacing the old guy.

A statue, but the Irish were outraged.
He'd sat in the rain seventy-eight years.
Seagulls had whitened his back a bit.
The museum folk took him in – both parts.
Spent fifty thou on a near head transplant.
Despite that he still looks like a wild gang
at Donnybrook Fair whacked his gentle soul.

-- Ann Curran

Catching the Blues

Once I went to sea
in a Jersey tub
that bounced in the waves
like a drunken cork,

spied on fish beneath.
We chugged for minutes,
then dropped all our lines.
I pulled in six sad

squirming, dying blues,
watched their quick gutting,
refused to claim mine.
Leaned over the side

to spit my gum,
and without a thought,
gave the survivors
my breakfast and lunch.

-- Ann Curran

Of A Transient Nature

Nearly every block there is a flower stall, offering
 blossoms
and greenery, fresh from the farm. Plants sprawl
over balconies in stacked apartments, reminders of home
perhaps, here in Buenos Aires. Not enough parks
 available
to keep millions satisfied. Creeping downward, plants
 shoot out
skinny arms, covering buildings with the gaudy grief

of graffiti. Boldly they add color to figures and shaped
 letters
registering protest after protest – the government and
 police
never stop. Entire sides of buildings splashed.
Public monuments tagged. It has become art. This
 mixture
of flowering and thin-boned black scratches. For tourists,
it is a shock to see vistas of marked buildings, several
 stories high.

It is protest in the most elemental style. And flower stalls
 keep selling
and people keep buying, taking it all. My daughter
 purchases a bouquet
of fresh gerbera daisies. I cut into an empty water bottle
with my nail scissors. How they brighten this drab room
 and clash
with the institutional orange bedspreads. I see in their
 petals
opportunity for language, how they could slip out

the window and crawl down the red neon sign of the
    Liberty Hotel.
One rainy morning, outside the hotel's front door, we
    notice
a plaque installed in the pavement beside the grubby man
who whisks sugared nuts all day in a big bowl.
According to the memorial, one afternoon a diplomat was
    snatched
from this spot and murdered. It lists names of others

killed right here, outside the door we step through
numerous times without a thought. Careless not to note
dun-colored flatness, framed by a border of red,
orange, and yellow tiles that will not wear out, no matter
how many feet stomp across it. Right here at *Calle Florida*
it would be easy to grab someone, force the prisoner into
    a cab

and race away. There are many ways of playing politics
in this city – corruption, thievery and even kidnapping are
    no big deal.
Discontent is like the heavy coats we shrug into, shadows
    lingering
close to the ground. Why not mark buildings with colored
    spray paint
or timeless black? Disharmony and causes. Flowers
for sale nearly every block in the city's true heart.

-- Virginia Chase Sutton

Roadtrip

I wonder where that splinter went that hurt for about a week, until it didn't.

The one you tried to take out, but couldn't. The one you thought you saw under the motel-lamp-light of seven different roadside rooms. One in Denver, two in Aspen, one in Vegas, and so on. The one in Vegas had a view of Paris showing itself to us from our Bellagio-Nevada window, snowless and short of Boulevards, no *en plein aire* paintings, though the impressionism was there, that's for sure – the copy of Elvis, the shadows of so many cities – all those mimics in the hot, red sun. Where did that splinter go? The one that pestered as I pressed the pedal and tried to keep a steady 70 towards California, the destination, finally – a long way from Miami; a long way from home. The place where you would leave me, let me go, leave another print that pressed on another impression. It's strange though, how that splinter hurt so much, and then, just a couple days after you left. It was gone. Swallowed by my foot, no more pain in my sole. No more callused sensitivity, no more watching where I stepped. Perhaps it dispersed into my new carpet. What a happy thought. Or, perhaps it was Puck, that schmuck, who sucked it out of me while I lay sleeping.

Or, perhaps it was something else, something much worse than all of that – because perhaps it is still making its silent drive, its intravenous joyride towards my heart. Piercing at once, once the only thing left of you is the dust you carried into my car seat's black, worn leather, which I haven't washed yet.

-- Vanessa Garcia

Lunar Winter

> "Europeans once thought swans and snow geese wintered on the moon." -- Annie Dillard

They must have witnessed
an ascending migration,
silhouettes rising
along a lunar trajectory,
imagining their pale grace
over the Sea of Tranquility:
swans casting long-necked shadows,
geese honking in victory flight,
their gossamer, slow-motion descent;
or, in free fall
like pieces of alabaster
into that windless world,
embossing starry craters
in ageless powder.

Discovering their wings inferior
to a new-found ability
to leap among the rocks
of this ghostly garden.
Surviving on starlight,
camouflaged against
all threat of discovery;
dreading its cold, new moon darkness,
rejoicing in its full moon warmth,
while looking back
at that marbled blue orb
and wondering whether
they'll be able
to find their way home
in time for spring.

-- Bill Carpenter

Flight

Seen through the tiny round-cornered window
the snowy north retreats
in a shawl of freezing haze
out from under the plane's left wing.
Beyond, fabled territories ghost by –
Nevada, Idaho, Montana, Saskatchewan.
It's hard enough to think of shearing thin air
in this big winged shiny tube
toward the wintry Right Coast,
when California still cups its temperate mouth
seductively to my ear.

From up here, the Sierra Nevada
bear their mountain name
                (Snowy Sawtooth)
                                with a vengeance.
Caped in blinding white on the first of March,
they gnarl out toward the four horizons
below the airplane's shadow,
a bunching, big-faceted
balky-knuckled crust,

punched up out of deep earth
by sex-mad spiny-backed prehistoric *things*
rearing with immemorial lust
for the top of the world.
Their frozen track,
a snarl of chalky snake bones
laid out over a vast land
still as death.

Higher than gods, we read the wooded slopes below
in texture only. Way too distant
to pick out whole trees
with roots that chew mountain talus
down to where coiled layers of the past
make living matter.

If we could hold to our airborne vector safely,
keep on and penetrate Earth's atmospheric envelope,
why not then delve back
into the haunted womb of time itself,
doggedly upstreaming
against the trail of light and life
toward Big Bang land
and whatever it was birthed from,
Before.

Come full circle,
shoot the Black Hole,
Mobius-stripping
into a haunt of elements
our evolved brains lack means to decode.

Pre-life.
Back of time,
          back
               to
                    Is.

-- Calvin Ahlgren

Cornelius and The Big Blow

"How cold was it?" Old Cornelius was serious.
He never read the paper or watched TV weather
news. His idea of forecasting was checking his
horse's coat or dipping both hands in vinegar,
standing on the chicken house, holding up his arms
till they froze, or were dust crusted.

Cornelius didn't have much up top, but he meant
well. Should a tornado threaten, he shoved each family
member, two cows, Henry, our sag-backed pony
and 17 chickens into the shelter. Goodhearted or not,
Dad finally talked the old man into leaving
the chickens outside.

Come a snow storm, Cornelius put up plenty
of guide ropes from house to barn to fence to pig sty,
back to the house, and finally to the root cellar. A person
couldn't get lost in blizzards at our place, but they risked
strangulation if they went out to milk cows.

Cornelius loved weather, the wilder the better.
One summer the wind blew off part of our windmill.
Next thing we knew, there was the old fellow, clinging
tight to the stem of the blades, mouthing nails, a huge
hammer in hand. We closed our eyes and prayed.

There came one day that Cornelius met his match weatherwise. We'd had a hot, dry summer. One morning we woke to a horrible crunching sound which means only one thing – locusts. Cornelius jammed on his hat and braved strong winds to do battle. He carried a large watering can filled with axle grease.

Poor Cornelius. He never got to use it – last we saw of him, the wind filled that can and he was blowing in a straight line toward the Kansas border. It was spring before we heard any word – the old man sent us a postcard from Florida where he had his eye on a big
    hurricane.

-- Gail Denham

Remembering Chief Charlie DePoe Who Loved Trains

"Charlie DePoe, a leading man among the Indians, was a chief of the Joshua tribe and was noted for his good sense and wise councils and hospitality among the Indians. No one ever went away hungry from the home of DePoe Charlie." -- *Lincoln County Leader,* July 12, 1918

Who knew train engines at Toledo
would harm the Pacific sky?

Maybe it was whiskey ingenuity
of Scots leaving ancestral ground

like a strange unnatural salmon
unable to find his way home

who pretended he didn't have one
and roamed open sea

until his belly grew so large
he devoured channel buoys,

then boats, and finally at high tide
entire coastal villages.

-- Scott T. Starbuck

Reading *Conquest of the Incas* in the Cirque,
    Central Peru

Have the dead always been so silent?
The syllables of these mountains
roll off the tongue like powder
shaken loose from a slope
too long exposed to the sun:
Chacraraju, Huascaran.
The slippery glide of a millrace.
But up there the only sound is absence.

The only shore a myth.

Wisps of cloud flit across the tip of Chacra.
Stones with gagged voices.
A moon stolen by smoke.
That glint in the rock a crushed spur.
Runners launched from Cuzco bear messages
from one end of the empire to the other.
Earthquake and avalanche,
aliens astride terrible mounts they call *horse* and *wheel.*
Dogs in the temples, the granaries.
The sun god melted into bars.

Everywhere frozen shadows.
Flame immune to water.

-- Peter Ludwin

Detour: Driving North on I-5

One March day you come upon a town
called, perhaps, Canyon Creek, deep
in Oregon's woods. You pass a house,
plain and white, white curtains
at the windows, white cat smiling in the yard,
small white daisies spreading through the lawn.
Along the path leading to the porch, iris leaves
jut up, sharp and bare. Suddenly you know
this is where Iris, messenger of gods, has gone;
and when she leaves, everywhere she steps
will bloom and this house and yard will melt
into a rainbow. You want to knock and shout
until she answers, to see her and confront her
in her golden wings and ask – oh so many things –
but do not dare, for Spring is not the only news she bears;
and you have much that waits behind your own front door.

-- Sheila Nickerson

Fire

Santa Ana winds ignited the grassy
hills behind our house that summer as
it did every summer. I was 17 and we were
recently divorced from my father. Smoke colored
our already-bruised California air.

My mother, unable to sleep one night, said let's
drive to Mexico to meet a friend even though
we'd heard the Ventura Freeway was closed.
Let's try anyway, she said, and that
was a beautiful thing to say.

Without moon or stars we made
our way south. Now and then
we'd slow as fire fighters waved
us on in a kind of benediction.
I was impatient to grow up and
my mother wished to be young
again. Together we urged our
old van down that haloed
freeway, faster and faster,
towards the possibility
of love.

-- Beth Hutmacher

We Did Not Come for the Birds

    We did not come for the birds, but the petroglyphs:
a rabbit with ears large enough to catch the wind,
the only rock rabbit in all of Wyoming, though yesterday
a live one planted itself in the snow outside the picture window.
It was so still I thought at first it was only an outline, the way
a shadow sometimes forms, as if the body had disappeared
or leaped from its silhouette, as when a girl leaps outside
the doubled ropes in a game of Chinese jump rope.

    The clouds forming into fists even before
the afternoon snow. Weather always unpredictable
here, where a morning begins bitter cold, then a warming
descends with planks of ice breaking off from the eves.

    Down by Cottonwood Creek in view of the petroglyph
figures with waving arms and the antelope prancing up the
    rocks
at a sharp angle, a band of rough-winged swallows
swooped in, just below where we perched studying the
    drawings.
The birds were agitated, alighting, pecking for bugs or seeds.
Off again, looping in a figure eight like a woman wrapping yarn
around the outstretched arms of a friend in a knitting club.

    They're all on those rocks: the turtle who dove to the
ocean bottom and surfaced with mud, the hump-backed
    flute player.
But the blur of birds is what I remember most, a grey mass
like a general's greatcoat flung over a puddle so a woman
could step on it and not ruin her pearl satin shoes.

    Only later, driving home over the Big Horn Mountains
the grey shape darkened to black; I catch a glimpse in the rear
view mirror, the Angel of Death hovering, trailing us
as the car swerved on the ice over the mountain pass.

-- Carol Davis

Leaving

The dead leave so quickly,
venturing to unmapped lands:
no ticket home,

no forwarding address.
Bravely they step from their bodies,
empty now and frayed at the seams,

ill-suited for the task at hand.
Resolutely, between our sobs,
they turn away from living.

The dead haven't time
to explain or console –
death is their final obligation

and they do it well,
trusting us to navigate
earth's corridors without them.

After they leave,
we vow to remember
every voice and deed, each touch –

to tease again the quiet magic
of their arms and legs.
We vow to light the chamber

labeled past and keep it bright,
but dear faces fade and merge
with shadows.

Some tap like lost moons
against our window glass
and then move on.

-- Diane Stone

Great Wave Off Oklahoma

   (Great Wave Off Karagama, Hokusai ~1832;
      Trail of Tears, President Andrew Jackson, 1832.)

Off in the distance
there is a sacred mountain,
comforting as prayer.

But here Old Hickory and carved cherry
woodblock prints are drunk on power:
waves dressed in blue
with white foam claws
wrenching them Indians from their longboats
to the earth, drowned.

They say *walk to that sunset, boy, and bleed
for our cowboy king.* Here, wood pulp, ink, and law, are air.

The ones pulled off the salty trails
are paved into the sea.

We mark the trail heads
with their jaw bones

so they can pronounce the bottom-most half
of what the eagles whisper, clutching arrows.

Cut up brother deer's fur for meat
to choke on. Wash the wolf's skin
so something here is clean. Flay the fish
down to the bone. Carve the flesh from
the Holly Leaves, remember a nose full of salt like snow.

Drift onto a wave breaking red
on Oklahoma shores.

Off in the distance
there is a sacred mountain,
wanting for comfort.

-- Michaelsun Knapp

V INTERIOR FRAMES

Adventure

I do not dream
of being launched
atop a rocket
to explore the heavens
and view the Earth
as a glittering marble.
I do not long to
snap on scuba gear and
dive into the ocean
to gaze eye-to-eye with
neon-colored creatures
of the Barrier Reef.
The thought of skiing
down double-black trails
in the Alps, or anywhere,
leaves me cold.
You'll never spot me
crouched on a surfboard
riding just ahead of
the crest of a monster
wave off the coast of Maui.
You can have rock
climbing with helmet,
hammer and pitons,
scaling sheer cliffs like
Yosemite's Half Dome.
I'll see it from the tour bus.
For adventure, I'll settle for
the nest of my easy chair
surrounded by some
needlepoint, a good book,
a challenging crossword puzzle,
and a sharpened pencil,
or, if I dare,
a pen.

-- Ann Boutte'

Housesitting on Looking Glass Lane

She has beheaded every rose;
tight red buds litter the lawn.
Their exuberance tattoos
hands and forearms.
She feels, somewhat, a Pict
in her polka-dot boots.
A mockingbird repeats:
rat tat ta toun-da …
from that Pink Floyd song
with the long title.
Flickering fluorescents
silver backs of her knees.
She moves as if underwater.
Butterflies loom, huge
threatening pterodactyls,
and flowers tall as trees
claw at her from nursery walls.
The dogs, hound and pit bull,
slaver exuberance, then fade.
All that remain are tongues
like soggy flannel blankets.
Perhaps, she's a dormouse
bereft of sugar bowl, and
the front door's oval glass
a portal. Nothing in the pantry
is labeled *Eat Me* or *Drink Me.*

-- Ann Howells

Boat Launch

Wherever all roads lead to,
it is not this sodden marsh
where egrets clump and moisten
the overhanging trees
and alligators, snide and side-eyed,
cut diagonals, up-snout a bit,
and swallow naïve dawdling ducklings.
Not here where only water laps, while
cicadas, night toads, and hosts
of thrashers, Carolina wrens, and varied anonymities
triple-tongue, burp, squeak, tweet,
way past last light.

Imagine yourself safely aboard a skiff, I say.
Once there, piloting casually,
hit or miss, embark on pumping out,
as you would any heavy rain,
the residue of desperate prayers, wild hopes,
bargains for dulled souls, vagrant murmurs,
double-crossed memories.
Float them upside down, sideways, inside out,
flotsam, jetsam, however you can.
Whistle like a bos'n.
Navigate, if only a few low-tidal feet,
or, grinning, slowly start to spin.

-- Pamela A. Smith

Yesterday's Light

> *We keep coming back to what we gave up*
> *Lisel Mueller*

So strong, this impulse,
to find the exact spot
near the swinging bridge
where the country store once stood.

The empty field owes me nothing.
I drive by slowly, follow
the river road and memories;
dark oiled floors, the fragrance
of blueberry buckle fresh
from the oven, a plump little woman,
housedress and apron, who stepped
from behind a curtained doorway,
scooped peach ice cream
on a summer day
sunlight muted through the maple.

This need to travel back
to find that depot of innocence.
The fifties steak house,
white and chrome and black;
its green awning long gone
the building now splashed
with garish red and yellow script
in a language I don't understand.
Near the heavy entrance door
I close my eyes, smell gardenia,
my prom date corsage,
picture the boy who pinned it on,
his eyes soft like brown velvet.

At the end of main street,
the fountain replaced
with a more efficient rotary,
stained glass windows
removed from the Spanish-style
church where, long ago,
friends gathered
to witness our wedding vows.

Now an arrow points
to the upper floor
and a neon sign flashes
in one of the clear window panes:
Tattoo Parlor –
the needle-prick of now,
the indelible imprint of then.

-- Lois Parker Edstrom

A Breath Before Doubt

I know. I'll surprise you and fly
    through the roaring redeye tunnel,
and let myself in by dawn,

so that you'll find me before you,
    before you can be sure
I'm there. You'll blink and wonder,

Wasn't the world still in the way
    last night? True. I stayed, and you,
rope of your work round your neck,

went. I know, the tug meant follow
    or choke. And wasn't I tied
by tough jute twine to my post?

But tonight, a sorcerer's dozen
    books beside me on the bed
where you'd sleep, the wind creeps

through the walls and windows, slips
    the knots, sets me loose to cross
through the dark's cloud-shot eye

the thousands of miles to your brow,
    your lips ... I'll watch you
smile, a breath before doubt,

as I kiss you unnoosed in the dim-lit
    spell of our touch, till quick
as a gust snuffs a candle out,

the dawn light disperses my flesh.

-- Jed Myers

Dutchman's Trail, Superstition Wilderness

The trail scarcely marked, each turn
takes us a little further into the unknown.
We talk, stepping carefully, negotiating
the uneven ground, the smooth bedrock
and broken sandstone.

Like small mysteries, the footfalls of another
become words: the occasional slip and regain
of balance, the emergent rhythm as one leads
and the other follows.

Today, I heard your voice. How it lifts
out of the silence, a sudden whirr of quail
flushed from hiding. Beautiful words
like cholla, saguaro, and ocotillo.

Today, I felt your silence. How it reflects
in the soft nubs of creosote, scent imprinting
the desert air. How it fills a shard of quartz
with a glint of happiness.

I could see, at times, through your eyes
the changing light, the approach of evening.
How blue the Sonoran sky can be.

-- John Baalke

Destination: The Fallow Land

Not left fallow;
Not resting, patient, ready to grow.
The hungry years.
And if the soil grows rich?
How savor the coming harvest,
With the belly empty, grumbling?
Ready to eat the vacant soil,
Rather than sow and reap and wait.

Who can survive the fallow years,
And learn to eat again?
The hand that stirs the dust
Raises the taste of dirt.
With nothing to risk, nothing to lose,
Nothing to fear from the absent rain.
How plant a crop, drag a plow?
How raise the ache of hope
From a barren stretch of ground?

What would grow?
Some twisted vine, fit only for climbing?
A berry patch, thick with briars and thorns?
Glowing mushrooms?
Stunted corn?
What appetite would be aroused?
Who would we be
after such a reckless planting?

-- Ilene Adler

Destination: The Fertile Land

Not by your own hand,
Or any other.
Not by the preparation of the soil.
Flowering out of rock or sand or
Jungle floor,
Simply because the time has come.
And the night sky is black
And pulsing with stars.

If there was a season for planting,
We never noticed.
We were too busy,
Hunting through the almanac.
Trying to find the clues
To wind and seed and weather.
And now, though we missed the spring,
And the rain never fell,
And all of nature is hopelessly
Out of pace with us,

Look what's grown.

-- Ilene Adler

Unlikely Journeys

When you were a child
you tossed a leaf, or a stick
into a swift river
to follow its journey.
You watched it tangle in debris,
spin and break away,
marveled as it dipped
beneath a backwash,
waited for it to surface
and navigate a field of boulders.
You cheered as it forged a narrow sluice
picked up speed with the approaching falls,
to disappear behind a curtain of foam
and bob to the surface in a rush of white water.
Astonished with its success,
you turned on it,
hurled stones to sink your creation,
that continued undaunted.
Angered, you tossed ever-larger rocks,
like the Cyclops raging against Odysseus,
as it drifted out of range.
Surrendering to its triumph
you shouted belated encouragements
as the vessel continued
toward a distant sea.

-- Bill Carpenter

Antelope Canyon, Arizona

The stocky Navajo collects his twenty dollars
and drives me the half mile to the site.
"I'll be back in an hour to get you," he says.

I'm left in a canyon of meandering walls
that never touch,
north male, south female,
its amber space sculpted by flash floods,
light falling in a curtain through the chink of sky
onto the image and its reflection,
one in light, the other in shadow,
a topaz split into a cubism of curved space.

Midway, I sit in a hollow,
between the halves of this petrified storm,
showered in a veil of sand,
that chimes like an inverted rain-stick,
as the wind whistles a serpentine song.

"Did you hear the walls talk?" my guide asks.
"I go to restore balance," he says,
"the walls absorb the world's 'twisted' energy,
and when enough of it is trapped,
the floods come to wash it away."

-- Bill Carpenter

Hiking with my Son in the Grand Canyon

He's twelve.
He's far ahead and
      far below, about to
             disappear.

He wants to get there fast
      and first.

I feel beneath my feet
         the drop of air between us.
He feels the path,
      the pull of his
           sure gravity
               toward the goal,
    leaning into it,
         the way the Colorado
       tumbles to the sea.

    Here
ravens ride the updrafts,
      effortless
          against gravity and time,
      layer by layer,
         winding upward
              toward the present.
Flowers
    lose their seed
           to ledges beyond,
       free of fear
            and afterthought.
I stand
    poised in this moment,
        massive cliffs before me,
              breathless body
        breathing.

-- Mark Hart

Story

I once traveled through the night on a train
and dreamed I was flying, hair pointing to stars.

In the morning the stranger who'd sat next
to me was gone, but I have remembered

all my life the warmth of his hand,
folded over mine like the wing of a bird.

-- Beth Hutmacher

Black Bear Hunt, Olympia, Washington

Bear scat lay everywhere
in that vast western forest –
beside fast-moving streams;
scattered among young fir trees
that covered the earth
like ferns;
and in the fall air, the nose-wrinkling
huskiness of bear.

After our hounds picked up bear tracks,
after we ran for hours behind them,
crashing through thick growth, smashing
shins on fallen logs,
after we were soaked in sweat,
our enthusiasm flagged, our legs
turned to rubber,

the bear so fast,
his stamina so great,
he could have outlasted us.
Day strained toward evening, the dogs
soon to tire.

Then steady barking signaled
the bear had treed,
and we stopped,
and crept forward,
and found him high in an old fir, his face
hidden in foliage,
his black fur nearly invisible
against dark branches.

My bullet
brought him tumbling from the tree.
We laid him out, stared.
He had only three legs,
the fourth a well-healed
stump.

The landscape spun. I closed
my eyes,
thanked him, begged
forgiveness,
cursed my own pierced heart.

My husband is gone now,
all excuses extinguished,
and the bear's head on my wall
is darkness.
When I awaken from dreams,
I am that darkness,
feet flying through the forest, determined
to live the only life I can.

-- Patricia L. Goodman

Dream on Aitutaki

Tethered by the leg to a coconut palm, a young
pig with no name rubs her back against the bark
by the turquoise water, the waves rolling in

do not give the pig a name
do not attach to beauty, I am told
beauty cracks the heart,
I am told you cannot slit the throat

when the pig's name sticks to your
tongue, you cannot hear the coconuts
fall, the wild roosters crow, you do not hear

me whisper your name

you drop the machete coated in coconut milk
rinsed by the rain now falling, wash the evidence

from your hands, drop
your eyes at sunset on the white sand
to the reflection of the vaca
black on the water, in the lagoon a ghost

paddle in hand, shadow of the butchered
animal at your knee, though you have
not spoken, you paddle north, to the open arctic water

where your ashes drift on the Kobuk River
mix with ice melt, permafrost, dissolve in

rising seawater. On the current I float closer to you
a quarter inch a year, to your voice silenced, to your mouth
growing gills, to the scales you shed on the rocks.
I forget beauty, your death, forget I am sea foam
algae, forget the simple organism floating on the surface

silent, incapable of pain.

-- Gretchen Diemer

On Transplanting the Popp[ies]

Savior has given me plant[s]
taken from his old house.
His wife has died and he i[s]
Poppies can go, too. Mari[e]
like that, roots being drive[n]
as if to a party. Marie would wear
a red dress and her lovely smile.
"Now Daddy," she would say to Savior,
"Be careful." If only we could
forget that Marie now lives
in a small box quietly by Savior's bed,
we would tell her how glad we are
once more to be traveling together
across town and time
to a place we've been invited
where we can bloom and touch again.

-- Sheila Nickerson

A Hui Ho

On this crossing, Mau'i to Moloka'i
in the wee hours, the vessel's engineer
reports *a little windy; we'll try
to quarter it,* he reassures me,
and the *Safari Explorer* slips
into Pailolo Channel with the roiling
blue stream of the Pacific rolling
through this eight-point-four-mile gap,
one of the windiest and roughest
in all the Hawai'ian Islands.
That is Pele's doing – two of Her
muscular emerald mountain islands
put a goddess's squeeze on the sea;
and I can almost see ghosts of whalers
making this passage with me, ones
singing old whaling songs to ukuleles
as the season's last *Megaptera novaeangliae,*
two humpbacks, mother and calf,
depart on their ancient watery way
to the high Arctic feeding grounds –
and we follow them on this ship
of my passing grief, while in tossing waves
I cast onto their moonlit surface
a few more gritty bits of bonedust,
what's left of my only brother.

The current takes him to the good place
where *Kanaloa* and his spouting beasts reign.

-- Karla Linn Merrifield

VI Arrival

In compiling this collection, I am greatly indebted to my colleague Victoria Simmons for her insightful readings and comments, and to Ann Brantingham for her help in cover design and general good advice.

Humble thanks go to all the poets in this book for their faith and trust in sending these word-pictures forth into the world.

VII Poet Notes

"But I was only a poet – that is to say, a maker of stone axes – and she felt a real pity for me because of it: what a shame that I hadn't lived back in the days when they used stone axes! And yet, why make them now?"

    -- Randall Jarrell, <u>Pictures</u> <u>From</u> <u>An</u> <u>Institution</u>

Judith Adams was born in Suffolk, England. Her poetry was featured in the anthology *The Poetry of Dogs,* published by J. A. Allen. Judith's poetry has been choreographed for performance in New York State. Her books include *Springing the Hill, Crossing the Line,* and *I wanna Die Nice and Easy;* also CD's and two children's books published by Wynstones Press in England.

Ilene Adler writes: I teach English at a Japanese cultural center in New York City and make the most of this cultural immersion. I recently completed my first memoir, *Read My Mind,* and am engaged in the search for a compassionate agent.

Calvin Ahlgren was born and raised in Tennessee, and migrated to the West Coast in the mid-60's for graduate school and then a career in print journalism. His work has appeared in various Marin Poetry Center anthologies, Blue Pen online journal, the West Marin Review and elsewhere.

Carol Alexander's poems have appeared in *Bluestem, Canary, The Commonline, Chiron Review, Illya's Honey, Mobius, Red River Review, Poetrybay, Poetry Quarterly, San Pedro River Review,* and *Sugar Mule,* and in the anthologies *Broken Circles, Joy Interrupted, The Storm is Coming, Proud to Be: Writing by American Warriors,* and *Surrounded: Living With Islands.* Alexander's chapbook *Bridal Veil Falls* is published by Flutter Press (March 2013).

A third-generation Washingtonian, **Gabrielle Baalke** makes the most of gray days, rain showers, low clouds and occasional sun breaks by living and working on Whidbey Island. Joining her in this pursuit are her husband, who is from Wisconsin by way of Alaska, and her cat, who is crazy.

John Baalke has an MFA from Seattle Pacific University, and has published poems and reviews in several journals. He spent many years living in rural Alaska, and more recently moved to Whidbey Island along with his wife and their crazy cat.

Linda Beeman is an award-winning poet living on Whidbey Island in Puget Sound. She is the author of *Wallace, Idaho*, a chapbook celebrating the history of her gritty, silver-mining hometown. Her poems are published in *Windfall* and *Raven Chronicles,* and online at the University of Chicago's *Euphony.* Linda's new book *Collateral Damage* is now available at: https://finishinglinepress.com/product_info.php?products_id=1977

Ann Reisfeld Boutte' is a writer of poetry, essays and feature stories. Her work has appeared in many publications. She has a Master's Degree in Journalism and has worked as a feature writer for a national news service. She was a Juried Poet in the Houston Poetry Fest in 2001, 2005, 2009 and 2010.

Catharine Bramkamp is a writing coach and podcaster. She has parented two boys past the age of self-destruction and has authored numerous works, including *The Real Estate Diva* mysteries, two essays in the *Chicken Soup for the Soul* anthologies, and the collection *Ammonia Sunrise.* She is the author of *Don't Write Like You Talk* and *The Cheap Retreat Workbook.* She is an adjunct professor of writing at University of Phoenix & JKF University. www.YourBookStartsHere.com and www.NewbieWriters.com.

Bill Carpenter writes: My poetry has appeared in *The Newport Review, Runes, Blueline, Chest, Balancing the Tides, July Literary Press, The Cancer Poetry Project, Write Wing Publishing* and the Rhode Island Writers' Circle. I'm a member of the Ocean State Poets, whose mission is to spread poetry throughout the community.

Ann Curran is the author of *Me First* (Lummox Press) and *Placement Test* (Main Street Rag). Her poetry has appeared in *Rosebud Magazine, U. S. 1 Worksheets, Blueline, Ireland of the Welcomes, Commonweal Magazine,* and elsewhere. She wrote for the *Pittsburgh Post-Gazette* and *Pittsburgh Catholic,* and edited *Carnegie Mellon Magazine.*

Carol V. Davis is the author of *Between Storms* (Truman State University Press, 2012). She won the 2007 T. S. Eliot Prize for *Into the Arms of Pushkin: Poems of St. Petersburg.* Twice a Fulbright scholar in Russia, her poetry has been read on NPR and Radio Russia, and at the Library of Congress. She teaches at Santa Monica College, California.

Margo Davis's poetry has appeared in *The Sow's Ear Poetry Review, A Clean, Well-Lighted Place, Louisiana Literature, Passages North, The Louisville Review, Lifting the Sky,* and *Calliope.* Poems are forthcoming in *The Midwest Quarterly* and *Out of the Depths.* Two poems appear in Write Wing Publishing's anthology *Surrounded: Living With Islands.* When not managing Library Services at a leading law firm in Houston, Margo focuses on film, poetry and literature.

For 35 years, **Gail Denham**'s poems, stories, news articles, and photos have appeared in national and international publications. Denham belongs to many state poetry associations. She leads writing and photography workshops. Denham's family is a great source of story/ poem ideas. Humor and nostalgia color most of her work.

Gretchen Diemer's first book *Between Fire and Water, Ice and Sky,* was published by NorthShore Press in 2008. She taught school in the Alaskan bush and presently teaches special education in Palmer, Alaska. She is at work on her second book, poems revolving around the death of her husband in 2009.

Gelia Dolcimascolo has been a Writing Tutor and *The Writers' Circle* facilitator for 25 years at Georgia Perimeter College. Her poems have been exhibited at the Dunwoody Library, Marietta-Cobb Museum of Art, and GPC's annual Celebration of National Poetry Month, *Visual Voices.* Gelia's poem "Solo" appeared in Write Wing Publishing's collection *Surrounded: Living With Islands.*

Lois Parker Edstrom is a freelance writer living on Whidbey Island. The natural beauty of the island inspires much of her work. Her chapbook *What Brings Us to Water* received the Poetica Publishing Company Chapbook Award in 2010. Her second collection, *What's To Be Done With Beauty,* was published by Creative Justice Press in 2012.

Brett Foster has published two poetry collections, *The Garbage Eater* (Triquarterly Books/Northwestern UP) and *Fall Run Road,* awarded Finishing Line Press's 2011 Open Chapbook Prize. His poems have appeared or are forthcoming in *Atlanta Review, Green Mountain Review, IMAGE, Pleiades, Poetry Daily, Poetry East, Raritan, Salamander, Seattle Review, Shenandoah,* and others. He teaches creative writing and Renaissance literature at Wheaton College.

Vanessa Garcia is a multi-media and cross-genre artist and writer. She has written and reported for various publications including *The New York Times, The LA Times, The Miami Herald, HowlRound, The Southern Humanities Review, The Art Basel Magazine,* and others. She is also a Huffington Post blogger. Her poems have appeared in *Damselfly Press* and the *Shady Side Review.*
www.vanessagarcia.org/about.php

Patricia L. Goodman, a widow, mother, and grandmother, holds a degree in Biology and spent her career breeding, training, and showing horses with her orthodontist husband. She now lives in Wilmington, Delaware, where she enjoys hiking, gardening, and photography, finding her inspiration in the natural world.

Mark Hart, a native of the Palouse region of eastern Washington State, lives in western Massachusetts, where he is a psychotherapist, the guiding teacher for a Buddhist community, and a religious adviser at Amherst College. His poetry has appeared in *Atlanta Review, RATTLE, Poetry East, Margie, Tar River Poetry* and *The Spoon River Poetry Review.* His first collection, *Boy Singing to Cattle,* won the 2011 Pearl Poetry Prize.

Ann Howells has edited the print poetry journal *Illya's Honey* for fifteen years and is taking it to an online format beginning in October 2013. Her work appears in *Calyx, Crannog, Free State Review, RiverSedge, Plainsongs,* and *Third Wednesday,* among others. Her chapbook *Black Crow in Flight* is from Main Street Rag.

Judith O'Connell Hoyer writes: I have had poetry published in the *Yale Journal for Humanities in Medicine, Boston Literary Magazine, Avocet,* a journal of nature poetry, *Still Crazy, poetrymemoirstory,* and the anthology *Surrounded: Living With Islands*. I also earned a third place poetry prize in the 2012 Massachusetts State Poetry Society's National Poetry Day Contests.

Beth Hutmacher writes: I have been a traveler myself, although I am now settled in Port Townsend, Washington. For as long as I can remember I have been a poet in my heart, but only recently have I begun to put my words and my memories onto the page. These words and memories now seem to just spill out of me.

Michaelsun Stonesweat Knapp is a Native American and a college graduate. He has been published in *The Broken Plate* (Indiana State University), *The Pacific Review, The Black Tongue Review,* and, once they see the folly of their ways, *The North American Review.* He ain't bad on the eyes, either.

Ellaraine Lockie has been awarded the 2013 Women's National Book Association's Poetry Prize and her tenth chapbook, *Coffee House Confessions,* released from Silver Birch Press. She teaches poetry workshops and serves as Poetry Editor for the lifestyles magazine *Lilipoh.* She is currently judging the Reuben Rose Poetry Competition for Voices Israel and the Tom Howard/Margaret Reid Poetry Contest for Winning Writers.

Peter Ludwin writes: My most recent book, *Rumors of Fallible Gods,* was twice a finalist for the Gival Press Poetry Award. For the past twelve years I've been a participant in the San Miguel Poetry Week in Mexico. My work has appeared in *Crab Orchard Review, Nimrod,* and *Prairie Schooner,* among other journals.

Debra Marquart is the author of four books, including *The Horizontal World,* which was awarded the 2007 PEN USA Nonfiction Award and an *Elle* Lettres Award. Marquart is the recipient of the 2013 Wachtmeister Award, an NEA Grant, and a Pushcart Prize. She is the director of the MFA Program in Creative Writing and Environment at Iowa State University. Her poetry collection, *Small Buried Things,* is forthcoming from New Rivers Press.

Joe Massingham was born in the United Kingdom but has lived the second half of his life in Australia. He has run his own writing and editing business, but retired early because of cancer and heart problems, and now spends his time writing poetry and prose and smelling the roses.

Karla Linn Merrifield has had 400+ published poems in dozens of publications and anthologies. Among her ten published books are *The Ice Decides: Poems of Antarctica* (Finishing Line Press) and the new *Attaining Canopy: Amazon Poems* (FootHills Publishing). Visit her blog at http://karlalinn.blogspot.com.

Jed Myers is a Philadelphian living in Seattle. His poems have appeared or are forthcoming in *Prairie Schooner, Nimrod International Journal, Barely South Review, Atlanta Review, Jabberwock Review, The Quotable, Grey Sparrow, Crab Creek Review, Off the Coast,* and elsewhere. Among his recent awards is the 2012 Mary C. Mohr Editors' Award from *Southern Indiana Review.*

A former Poet Laureate of Alaska, **Sheila Nickerson** lives in Bellingham, Washington. Her poems have been widely published in magazines, chapbooks, and anthologies, including *Surrounded: Living With Islands.* Her nonfiction works include *Disappearance: A Map* and *Midnight to the North.* Her study of 19th century sledge dogs in the Arctic, *Harnessed to the Pole,* will be published by the University of Alaska Press in April 2014.

Barbra Nightingale has published eight books of poetry, and over 200 poems in various journals and anthologies. She is a senior professor of English at Broward College in Ft. Lauderdale, Florida.

Teddy Norris is a retired Professor of English who lives and writes in St. Charles, Missouri. She is a former editor of *Mid Rivers Review,* and her poetry has appeared in various journals, including *Untamed Ink, Cuivre River Anthology, Off Channel, Soundings Review,* and *Country Dog Review.*

Nasus is the pen name for **Susan Terhune Nunn**, a writer who writes first drafts with pencil and paper. She was a stewardess in the days when flying was a pleasant event, not an ordeal. Nasus is a Coupeville resident; her favorite pastimes include volunteering for Admiralty Head Lighthouse, writing poetry, and taking quiet walks.

Suzanne Ondrus's poems have appeared in *Slab, Frigg, Colere, JENDA,* the *LaLorna Anthology* and the Romanian journal *Nazar Look.* Recent work is in *Bohemia, Route7, NerdWallet* and *Long River Review.* She is an editor of *The Chagrin River Review.* Suzanne holds an MFA from Bowling Green State. Her book *Passion Seeds* won Little Red Tree's 2013 Venice Quebodeaux "Pathways" Poetry Prize for Women. She has lived and worked in Uganda, Burkina Faso, Russia, Benin, Italy, and Germany.

Marianne Patty writes: I am a poet and visual artist working in collage and colored pencil. I relate poem-making to collage, putting words down, taking them out, and moving them around. My poetry appeared in *Poetry of the Golden Generation Volumes III and IV,* and I was awarded third prize in the 2007 James Hearst contest. I was a *North American Review* finalist in 2011, and won Honorable Mention in the 2013 *Passager* poetry contest.

Pamela Smith is the author of twelve books, including two recent works of poetry, *Salmos from South Bethlehem* (Trafford, 2012) and *How Jonathan Green Painted My Momma* (Finishing Line Press, 2013). She was a contributor to Write Wing Publishing's previous anthology, *Surrounded: Living With Islands.*

Scott T. Starbuck's newest books are *River Walker,* a collection of Pacific Northwest fishing poems, published by Mountains and Rivers Press, and *The Other History, or unreported and underreported issues, scenes, and events of the 19th, 20th, and 21st Centuries* (November 2013, FutureCycle Press). He blogs at riverseek.blogspot.com. Website: http://www.pw.org/content/scott_starbuck_1

Diane Stone is a former technical writer-editor who lives on Whidbey Island in Washington. Her work has been published in *5 A.M., Rattle, Comstock Review, Soundings Review, Pontoon,* and other publications. She learned poetry from her grandfather, who taught her that poetry happens everywhere.

Russ Stratton was born in Makaweli, Kauai, 1938, educated at Princeton, once coached a Davis Cup team (not in this country), and had a long career in education but is now retired and very happily out of that byzantine world. He spends his days listening to Verdi and Mozart, gardening, drinking Tanqueray martinis, and with his wife of 44 years, admiring their three cats.

Virginia Chase Sutton's book *What Brings You to Del Amo* won the Morse Poetry Prize (UP of New England). Her first book is *Embellishments* (Chatoyant). Five times nominated for a Pushcart Prize, her poems have appeared in *Paris Review, Ploughshares, Antioch Review, Boulevard, Western Humanities Review, Witness,* and many others.

Ron Thompson is a caregiver, an assistant to people with the perplexities of disabled lives. Experimental artist and writer, his play "The Abrupt Edge of Reality" involved a cast of dozens and played to a rowdy SRO crowd. He continues to boldly attempt gardening in the foothills of Washington's Cascade Mountains. Ron's poetry appears in *Surrounded: Living With Islands.*

K. Andrew Turner writes literary and speculative fiction and poetry, and dabbles in nonfiction as well. He is a creative mentor, freelance editor, creative writing teacher, and managing editor of *East Jasmine Review.* www.kandrewturner.com

Rosemary Volz was born in Brooklyn, New York. She graduated from Queens College with degrees in Creative Writing and Journalism. At Queens she won numerous writing awards. Her short stories appear in *Blueline, Event,* and *Another Chicago Magazine.* Her poetry appears in *Evening Street Review, Earth's Daughter, Surrounded: Living With Islands, Conversations Across Borders, Baseball Bard, Pinyon,* and *Third Wednesday.* Rosemary works with the Tomoka Poets and lives in Ponce Inlet, Florida.

VIII About Write Wing Publishing

Founded in 2009 by Sheryl Clough, Write Wing Publishing offers editing, proofreading, and publishing services to the Whidbey Island / Western Washington writing community. Write Wing also seeks to promote poetry through publishing the work of poets at all stages of their writing experience. This collection is the second book by Write Wing; the first, *Surrounded: Living With Islands,* appeared in 2012.

When asked why poetry is important to society, the poet Sandra Ervin Adams responded: "Poetry is from the heart, and is therefore, a way to express feelings and emotions which need to be communicated in order for more peace, harmony, and understanding in today's world." In furtherance of this response, readers are encouraged to attend readings, buy books from poets, and support independent presses and bookstores.

Sheryl blogs once in a while at:
http://Scatchetpoet.blogspot.com

Made in the USA
San Bernardino, CA
18 February 2014